U MYAT THU AUNG

14 Articles on Non-Financial Aspects of Business, Mostly Marketing

Copyright © 2024 by U Myat Thu Aung

All rights reserved. Apart from personal use as well as fair use and library lending, all other uses require the prior permission of the author in writing. It is against the compliance of copyright laws to copy this book, post it to a website, make it available on the internet, or distribute it by any other means without the permission. Any support of the author's rights is highly appreciated.

First edition

This book was professionally typeset on Reedsy. Find out more at reedsy.com

TO MY PARENTS who have brought me to the world successfully, who have nourished me, who have provided me with necessities and non-necessities, who have protected me since my birth through my childhood and beyond, who have nurtured me in finest maternal manners, and who have helped me grow up in many different good ways.

*****

TO MY TEACHERS who have existed like a mountain in life and whose teachings have occupied in the chambers of my heart.

Contents

The Breeze of Globalisation	1
Relationship Marketing in the Digital Era	5
Consumer Buying Behaviour in the Modern World	10
Favourable Atmosphere for Inbound Marketing	13
Agile Marketing at a Single Glance	16
Preliminary Initiation of Market Entry into an Overseas...	18
Four Market Entry Methods for Market Development Strategy	23
One Indication of Lagging Behind	28
Stakeholders and a Change Project	31
Social and Cultural Considerations of Conducting Business	41
Preliminary Initiation of Developing a Sustainability...	48
Corporate Social Responsibility Models	51
Common Business Ethical Theories: A Snapshot Overview	56
Subtle Influences on Making Ethical Business Decisions	59

The Breeze of Globalisation

Imagine that a company boasts a successful history with its various flagship products; they all have gained tremendous success nationwide for at least a decade. In this scenario, the products must have entered maturity, leading to a proportional decrease in demand to a decrease in profit margin. Maturity is the third stage of Raymond Vernon's product life cycle after having progressed the earlier stages *Introduction* and *Growth* successfully, being its next and last stage is *Decline* in the cycle. At the stage of maturity, the decrease in sales for the products is significant enough and has been persistent for a long time. Under this condition, the products may enter – but not immediately – the *Decline* stage of the cycle at which there would be no profit enough to continue but gradually withdraw the presence of the products from the market in which the company operates. If the main reason behind this is because there is very little or no demand for any product which is similar in any degree to the products that the company offers, then it means that they have naturally reached the end of product lifecycle in the existing market. However in the age of globalisation, a product having finished its lifecycle in one market does not imply that it has finished the lifecycle in another market unless the demand for it has phased out globally. Thus, the company may market its products in a new market overseas where there remains considerable demand for the products. This is referred to as the market driver of globalisation.

Undeniably, technology also drives globalisation by means of instant communication and seamless information exchange, thereby increasing interconnectedness in the world. This connectivity brings people from different parts of the world closer, being one of the main features of globalisation. In fact, connectivity makes the world a global village where one can interact with another easily and instantly — just like in a village. This helps businesses a great deal because they can leverage established connectivity in creating interactions with a goal of converting them into transactions as many as possible. Besides connectivity, technology has also made the availability of e-commerce platforms and digital payment systems, enabling consumer access to products and services in international markets over the internet. In the absence of technology, globalisation can go on but in a limited way. Should technology not drive globalisation, economies would be limited to a regional level due to limited and weak interconnectedness and the flow of information would be slower in a restricted manner. Thus, technology has been not only a pivotal driver but also the essence of globalisation.

Another driver of globalisation is a monetary driver, leading to conducting business overseas. Now suppose that the company has other products that are at the Growth stage of Raymond Vernon's product life cycle and can make use of a good chance to launch them successfully in an overseas market which is highly relevant to them. If the company makes this decision based on the thorough evaluation of several factors relevant to this context, it could lead to steady increase in its profit – for example – by striving for lower costs for production, labour, resources, et cetera. Sometimes, one may be the first among its competitors to be there. Sometimes, one may tag along behind its competitors due to the competition: take Pepsi and Coca-Cola for example. If Pepsi is available in a certain country, Coca-Cola is supposed to be available there and is highly likely to soon arrive in that particular market so as not to get behind the competition, and vice versa. Thus, competition is also a driver of globalisation.

Reversely, globalisation also leads to increased competition despite the fact that competition itself is a driver of globalisation. When, for instance, Kentucky Fried Chicken (KFC) enters a new market, local suppliers of the same kind often vigorously compete with one another to get a lucrative deal with KFC. Moreover as abundant job vacancies progressively become available for a certain period in the respective local job market upon its market entry, there would also be a rise in competition there. These few examples indicate that competition can get intensified, whether slightly or greatly, because of one more new business in a market by means of globalisation. In fact, globalisation brings in a great number of new businesses to each market all over the world every year, potentially accompanied by the stronger intensity of competition of many kinds.

Impacts of globalisation on competitive landscape should be carefully recognised. Because of globalisation, similar businesses could become available more and more in a market, potentially leading to market saturation over a long period of time. Whether the market revenue may increase due to the rising number of businesses is not certain. But if the market revenue did not increase significantly enough in proportion to the number of all businesses operating in the same market, they would be unable to generate the same amount of revenue they used to achieve because all have to share the non-decreasing market revenue. It is simple mathematics. If a numerator p is divided by a bigger denominator q, one would get a smaller number r compared to a greater number z that would be obtained when the same numerator p is again divided by a smaller denominator k than q: take 5 ÷ 16 = 0.3125 and 5 ÷ 8 = 0.625 for example. Likewise if the non-increasing market revenue (p) is divided by the increasing number (q) of total similar businesses in the market, then each business could/would generate the lesser revenue (r) than it used to after the market has saturated and the market revenue has increased no more.

Relationship Marketing in the Digital Era

There is a transactional value when there is a transaction, thereby forming a mild relationship between a customer and the business. Upon purchase, customers gain functional utility and emotional utility as a transactional value derived from consuming the product purchased or utilising the service purchased. As for businesses, they gain an amount of money charged for their product sold and/or services provided as a transactional value. This is referred to as a marketing exchange, involving an exchange of a transactional value. Since there are no other values than a transactional value embedded in such a relationship, it could wither quickly unless it is further nurtured. To prolong it, a transactional value should be made superior to the extent that customers are willing to exchange commitment such that they would offer brand loyalty in the form of commitment in exchange for a superior value as the demonstration of commitment from the brand.

Relationship marketing can healthily facilitate an exchange process such that a chance to take place a successful marketing exchange is optimised. It works on developing relationships with customers and maintaining them, fostering customer loyalty so as to retain customers as long as possible and expecting recurrent transitions as many times as possible. In a nutshell, relationship marketing focuses significantly more on relationships with customers than on initiating one-off transactions. All relationships may come with a value of any degree: a relationship with a loyal customer holds a high value; one with a relationship seeker holds a moderate value paired with a high potential to turn into a high value; one with a one-time customer holds a low value; and one with an exploitative customer holds a least value. *Vertically* the higher the level of a relationship is, the greater the relationship value is; *horizontally*, a longer-term relationship has a greater relationship value than a shorter-term relationship. Being customer-centric regardless of relationship value can drive business growth and customer loyalty, prioritising the satisfaction of any customer and focusing more on creating optimal experiences for them instead of the focus on what benefits the business in the short term.

Customer bonding is a pivotal pillar of relationship marketing; its marketing activities are directed towards creating connections with customers and making them feel connected to the brand so as to be helpful in developing long-term, sustainable relationships. Nowadays, the increasing use of digital technology helps strengthen customer bonding stronger, bringing customers closer to businesses which recognise the power of social networks and leverage digital marketing as much as possible. Digital technology has influenced people to the extent that it affects the way consumers communicate and perceive. Becoming digital-friendly, people are widely accessible on digital channels – such as emails, social media, and messaging apps – where businesses can not only reach consumers digitally by targeting a specific audience as intended but also make themselves available to their customers and consumers at any time. As a matter of fact, there is no better time than now to leverage social media. A slim majority of today's consumers can be assumed that they rely on digital content for information. Businesses should therefore have a significant online presence over the internet for the accessibility and transparency of information as well as for better responsiveness in a practically short time. Communication which encourages interactions and lets exchange of experience is a key to customer engagement, potentially leading to initiating a relationship and then building it successfully. Without communication, no relationship will come into existence on its own.

By using software empowered by digital technology, businesses can effectively manage communication and customer interactions on multiple channels and at touchpoints. Adopting multichannel integration can give customers an ability to interact with them through various channels. Besides managing customer interactions, the purpose of multichannel integration is to have one integrated view of customers by compiling information on its customers across the various channels in use in order to better understand their customers and supports relationship marketing in strengthening relationships with customers. Although the primary focus of relationship marketing is on existing customers, multichannel integration enables anybody to choose how and when they interact with businesses. The tactic in this regard is: be available upon contact and be responsive as swiftly as possible. This implies that businesses should be available on many possible channels where their customers and prospects can be, and also keep an eye on all of their channels in place so as to respond in a timely and useful manner. Installing chatbot automation on digital channels in use has also become common, so there can be instant interactions with customers around the clock. Although this adds a value to customer service, robotic responses can frustrate customers instead of enhancing customer satisfaction unless automated responses are designed to be as human-alike as possible.

Owing to digital technology, it is now possible to collect customer data more than ever and hence more measurements of engagement can be available. Metrics data such as website traffic, website surfing behaviours, even the clicks on social media buttons (like button, share button, etc.), response times, and comments on social media can be collected, so customer engagement can be measured more effectively. Social listening tools are also available to keep track of what customers are speaking about products and services of their interest, which not only helps businesses observe customers' unsatisfied needs and learn what customers want better but also facilitates the development of relationships with their customers. To maintain and enhance relationships, accepting feedback and positively responding to them are helpful. With the help of digital technology, collecting or receiving feedback has become easier as consumers and customers can nowadays easily provide feedback online or on social media. It is critical that businesses manage, at least positively respond to, feedback properly upon the receipt. Studies found that customers are more likely not to repurchase if feedback left on social media is left unresponsive, thus feedback management should be not only given committed effort but also considered as a part of relationship marketing.

Above all, trust is a necessity in relationship marketing. Trust must tag along with any relationship which has come into existence, else it will be meaningless like food without salt is tasteless. In order to initiate a trust building process, businesses first have to demonstrate their trustworthiness as well as support customers in advancing to a higher level of trust towards them. Consumers should in turn attempt to correctly recognise their demonstration without any bias. When there is trust between businesses and their customers, commitment to each other reciprocates. Being a fundamental component of long-term relationships, trust not only makes sure there is no disconnection in relationships but also fosters loyalty and creates emotional bonds. Relationships based on reciprocal trust are effectively healthy and can extend their duration as long as possible. Relationship marketing relies on relationships, and trust fulfils by bonding relationships to be stronger.

Consumer Buying Behaviour in the Modern World

The internet and social media have led to a significant change in the way consumers make a decision to purchase, enabling consumers to have easy access to information online. So, consumers today are more informed and discerning. They now have more control over what, when, and how they purchase than ever before. One of the prominent consumers' buying behaviours is that they surf the internet and/or go on social media to search for the information and convince themselves before making a purchasing decision, including making good use of peer-to-peer feedback, online reviews, testimonials, and referrals. This indicates that consumers today would like to be corroborated, preferring to have known about products and/or services of their interest. It is referred to as Zero Moment of Truth (ZMOT). In the meantime, they also have multiple points of influence such as celebrity influence, word of mouth, and social online/offline networks. Nevertheless, this does not mean that consumers are not likely to be influenced by sales personnel and advertisements. At the contemporary time, consumer buying behaviour is seen as linear or sometimes cyclic. When consumer buying behaviour is linear, consumers pace towards an act of purchase step by step. Take the AIDA purchase funnel for example, where AIDA stands for Awareness, Interest, Desire, and Action. It sequentially involves steps towards a buying decision and purchasing such that consumers become aware of a product or a service through advertising and word of mouth, show their interest in it, express desire for it, and eventually purchase it. It is a progressive process from which at any stage consumers can disengage themselves for any reason. When a transaction happens, consumer buying behaviour associated with the purchase tends to transition from being linear to cyclic if customers experience it positively. Upon purchase, customers reflect and evaluate past experiences such as product /service performance, customer service, brand experience, and so on. Based on the evaluation, they would consider whether to repurchase from the same brand next time they need/want the same or something similar. This is referred to as cyclic customer buying behaviour. It is fairly common that some customers doubt whether they made a right buying decision regarding the purchase, potentially experiencing psychological discomfort. They tend to make attempts to ease the discomfort as much as they can, including cancellation, returning goods, seeking customer support, expressing dissatisfaction on social media, and so on. Unless the discomfort goes away, customers may seek alternatives next time or switch brands. Whether consumer buying behaviour is linear or cyclic also depends on the nature of products. Consumer buying behaviour towards products and/or services that have the recurrent nature influenced by ongoing or regular needs, routine, habitual usage, etc. tends to be cyclic. Take subscription services and consumables for example. If the nature of products and/or services are non-recurrent and infrequent, then consumer buying behaviour towards them is linear. Examples include repair services, durable goods, luxury goods, high-ticket items, and so on. Therefore, marketers usually approach consumer buying behaviour with a transactional approach if it is linear, and with relationship marketing if it is cyclic. Post-purchase behaviours often follow a purchase regardless of whether consumer buying behaviour has been linear or cyclic, including repeating purchases, seeking customer support, leaving reviews over the internet and on social media, spreading word of mouth, making referrals, or discouraging others to purchase.

Favourable Atmosphere for Inbound Marketing

Regardless of whether inbound marketing or outbound marketing, both involve activities of presenting and advertising products and/or services in different ways. The most significant difference is: inbound marketing attracts, engages, and delights potential and existing customers by providing useful content and creating positive experiences for them, whereas outbound marketing pushes marketing messages to broad audiences and makes efforts to get products and /or services in front of consumers regardless of their interest. There has been all over the world the widespread adoption of inbound marketing in line with the increasing global population of tech-friendly generations and the rising number of internet users worldwide, which slowly but steadily erodes traditional ways of marketing. Social media and the internet have significantly been a transforming factor in the marketing environment, making marketing become less challenging but more competitive. Since then, outbound marketing has no longer been a predominantly popular option for marketers because inbound marketing has become an irresistible option for more effectiveness with cost-efficiency as well as easier coordination of marketing activities on social media and over the internet. One study conducted in 2018 at Clark University's School of Professional Studies showed the following[1]: Inbound leads, i.e. leads which come from inbound marketing, cost less than outbound leads by almost two thirds on average; inbound marketing is 10 times more effective for lead conversion than outbound marketing if conducted properly; inbound marketing yields triple more leads for each dollar spent, compared to traditional methods which are also applied to outbound marketing. This indicates that inbound marketing performs better than outbound marketing at generating leads. Modern consumers also tend to respond better to inbound marketing because it is less intrusive, permission-based, and value-oriented (i.e. focusing on creating value for customers). Moreover, inbound marketing is compatible with Search Engine Optimisation (SEO) in a way that content used for inbound marketing in attracting consumers can be made search-engine optimised for more discoverability when internet users search on browsers. SEO is useful to inbound marketing for driving organic traffic by providing right content for those who are already searching for what they are interested in; inbound marketing can be more effective if search intent behind making queries can be understood better and as closely as possible. Besides SEO, widespread availability of many channels also enables business organisations to be on multiple channels which are relevant to their audiences in order to facilitate inbound engagements. Although current conditions are more favourable for inbound marketing to thrive on, outbound marketing has

---

[1] Assiriyage, Hasini; Zoeckler, Isabelle; Aghado, Emmanuel; Bu, Kefu; Jiang, Xiouyu; Kamble, Rajesh; and Wang, Yan, "Inbound Marketing" (2018). School of Professional Studies. 29. https://commons.clarku.edu/sps_masters_papers/29

remained relevant to this day. Perhaps in the future, conditions may change in a way that is again more favourable to outbound marketing.

Agile Marketing at a Single Glance

Marketing is not a monkey; yet how can it be agile? When principles of agile project management are applied to marketing practices, a marketing project is coordinated such that it is broken down into smaller parts comprising manageable tasks which can be completed for each part over a period called a sprint. The work completed at the end of each sprint is then reviewed before moving onto the next part of the project, being subjected to adaptation as necessary. This is referred to as an agile marketing project. What is special about agile marketing is quick, adaptive responsiveness to market changes such as emerging trends and competitor actions, timely executing marketing campaigns with agility in a flexible fashion. An ulterior tactic behind this is utilisation of market intelligence out of data obtained from keeping a close watch on the market, so no sooner are changes detected in the market than marketing responses can be given timely. Based on the market intelligence, marketing experiments are carried out such that their outcome(s) can be evaluated and refined each time in an iterative process. This is known as the test-and-learn tactic. Continuous improvement is the key feature of agile marketing, measuring the effectiveness of marketing activities having been carried out and incrementally improving results delivered each sprint. Agile marketing is often a preferred choice because it is useful for diversifying marketing costs and supports cost-effectiveness. However, agile marketing would be ineffective in the event of insensibly adapting in response to market changes which are not significant enough. Otherwise, it can be like a monkey randomly swinging from one tree to another without resting.

Preliminary Initiation of Market Entry into an Overseas Market

One common reason why companies consider entering an overseas market is because they would like to pursue strategic growth opportunities there by means of international expansion. In the event of entering an overseas market into which a company has not ever entered before, such a market is considered new to the company. In terms of growth strategy according to Ansoff Matrix, either market development strategy if the company intends to offer its existing products there or diversification strategy if the company intends to offer new products there should be considered. As for the risk associated, market development strategy is considerately less risky than diversification strategy being a substantially risky endeavour. Based on the strategy adopted for market entry into an overseas market, it is necessary that market research is undertaken in search of potential market opportunities there. Market intelligence concerning the market may be readily obtained and compiled, but specific market research may need to be carried out for questions which cannot be answered with the available market intelligence and hence need specific answers[2].

Depending on the nature of questions to be addressed, quantitative research, qualitative research, or a combination of both may be used. Quantitative research involves gathering quantifiable data and performing data analysis specific to marketing. It is particularly useful in testing a hypothesis, using sampling and statistical techniques. Thus, it usually requires data collection and hence involves consumer surveys to collect quantifiable data so as to analyse and express in a numerical language. The main goal is to eventually extract useful information. If, for instance, a company would like to know whether or not local people prefer online delivery service, it may conduct a survey about it and do quantitative analysis on the collected data. In constructing questions, they should be as specific as possible. As much as the accuracy of research findings is important, they need to be interpreted literally as they are. Suppose that the research finding for a survey question "Do you prefer delivery service for groceries?" is that 68% of the survey participants answer yes. However, this does not mean that the remaining 32% prefer otherwise such as order pick-up, in-store shopping, et cetera. In fact, quantitative research is simple enough as long as data collected is quantifiable. By quantifiable, it means that data collected can be measurable, expressed in numerical terms, and/or assigned numerical values. The use of qualitative data in quantitative research is very limited but challengingly possible if qualitative data points can be assigned numerical values. When the nature of questions is not simple enough, qualitative research should be considered. With the use of open-

---

[2] A list of typical market research questions for a target market overseas is provided as an example on the next page that follows the last paragraph.

ended questions in place of structured response, it involves subjective observation and collects non-numerical information during interviews with selected participants on a particular topic of interest. It aims to address complex questions that cannot be covered by quantitative research. In fact, qualitative research can be complementary to quantitative research; for instance, qualitative research can be carried out for generating a hypothesis which is then to be tested by qualitative research.

Sometimes, it is not easily possible for international companies to conduct market research overseas on their own due to common challenges including but not limited to the following: too many hypotheses to test, having time constraint or being time-consuming, cost inefficiency, inaccessibility of prospect targets, and extremely limited reach to a certain segment of the market. In this case, they should consider hiring a market research company/firm that is familiar with the local market for which market research is needed.

With the information obtained from the market research, it is recommended that an analysis of the competitive environment is conducted by adopting Kenichi Ohmae's 3 C's model. Also known as the strategic triangle, three C's stands for Company, Consumers, and Competitors. Mapping the relations between one another, this model optimises the balance of the strategic triangle such that the company leverages its strengths plus internal capabilities in serving consumers and customers as best as possible while outperforming its competitors. Where the three C's meet, there would be a price war, i.e. a tactic of continuously lowering prices in competition to gain more market share with greater customer attraction. For the gain of competitive advantage, there would be a race between the company and its competitors in meeting the needs and preferences of consumers and/or in fulfilling consumer wants so that one who outperforms the others in many aspects can achieve superior profitability and establish a stronger market position.

* * *

Examples of market research questions for a target market overseas, to be referred as the market below, include the following but not limited to:

- What is the current size of the market? Is the size big enough and/or worthy of entering?
- What is the projected growth rate of the market over the next one hundred months?
- What are the key demographic characteristics of the market?
- What are common purchasing habits in the market?
- How do people commonly make purchasing decisions in the market?
- What values do consumers in the market generally seek in making purchasing decisions?
- Are there underserved segments in the market? What needs are currently unmet?
- What other consumer needs than basic necessities for survival and well-being are common?
- What social and cultural values influence consumer behaviours in the market?
- How well do the value propositions align with the needs and preferences of various consumers in the market?
- How would consumers perceive the value of goods offered and/or services offered in the market in relation to their prices?

- What strategies regarding sales, marketing, and communication are common and effective in the market?
- How is the competition in the market?
- What are barriers for a foreign entrant to the market?
- Is the economy that governs the market stable? What about its key economic indicators?
- What are legal requirements for operating in the market?
- How is innovation in the market? To what extent technology is adopted in the market?
- What are strengths and weaknesses of the market? What about threats to the market?

Four Market Entry Methods for Market Development Strategy

Suppose that a company has been successful nationwide and it is financially safe to launch its existing products in a certain market which is new to the company by adopting a market development strategy regarding the market entry. In this scenario, the following are four relevant market entry methods in line with the market development strategy: franchising, joint venture, strategic partnership, and foreign direct investment.

Franchising is a special form of licensing. As for licensing, licensors permit another business or company to use the brand name in relation to its products and/or services. Licensees agree to pay licence fees in return for a licence permit. Particularly speaking, franchising is more complex than licensing. Franchising involves putting all elements together into a formula that makes the success of the products and/or services of a franchiser in its original market(s) and shares it with the franchisee upon purchase. Adhering to the franchise system agreed, the franchisee is granted the permission for use to operate the business under the brand name of the franchiser. Nonetheless, this does not mean that the franchisee will own the products franchised and/or services franchised. The franchisor receives franchised payments including royalties from its franchisees despite not involving in the operations of the business franchised. There is no limit to the number of franchisees a franchisor can have all over the world as long as it can oversee them effectively. However, having too many franchisees without an effective franchise system is too close to a chance that one of the franchisees might badly malfunction and happen to ruin the reputation of the franchisor. In practice, franchising may not be as simple enough as it sounds.

Joint venture is a business arrangement between two or more business organisations that come together to undertake a mutually beneficial project, potentially involving the creation of a new entity depending on its nature. Each party agrees to provide resources in undertaking the project with the aim to gain mutual benefits. Take the joint venture between Bayerisch Motoren Werke AG (BMW) and Brilliance Auto for example regarding BMW's foreign market entry into China. BMW was actively attempting to expand its presence in China, but navigating the complexities of its automotive market is challenging for a new entrant. BMW recognised strategic importance and the need of a local partner for thriving in China's automotive market which is one of the largest and fastest-growing markets globally, so it established the joint venture with Brilliance Auto by creating a new entity named BMW Brilliance Automotive Ltd. It has been largely successful, achieving substantial growth and profitability.

What slightly resembles joint venture is strategic partnership. It is a co-operative arrangement typically between two business organisations such that they work together towards mutual benefits, not necessarily needing to create a new entity. Take Kentucky Fried Chicken (KFC) and soft drink companies for example regarding strategic partnership. Soft drink is complementary to fried chicken. KFC customers prefer soft drinks while having fried chicken. Hence, KFC makes a strategic partnership with soft drink companies (The Coca-Cola Company, PepsiCo Inc., etc.) such that soft drinks are available for sale in its outlets. In this way, both parties benefit mutually. As for KFC, it can maximise its turnover and satisfy its customers. As for soft drink companies, they gain a lucrative deal for supplying vast volumes of soft drinks as a regular supplier to KFC. Like so, strategic partnership with a local partner that can be complementary to the company is a good option in the event of launching its existing products and/or services in an overseas market into which it has not yet entered before. It is often a more convenient entry method.

Another market entry method is foreign direct investment. When an investor from a country directly invests in foreign companies and/or assets located in another country, such investment is referred to as foreign direct investment or FDI. It typically involves acquiring a significant stake in at least one company incorporated in a foreign country such that there can be control or substantial influence over the company. If, for instance, a company plans to launch its existing products overseas that have gained tremendous success nationwide in its home country, it may look for domestic companies in another country that not only offer closely similar products but also are looking for foreign investment in exchange of ownership interest. In this way by acquiring the shares such that they are collectively dominant enough to control or exert substantial influence, the company can make direct foreign investment in line with the intention of entry into the local market in which its investee company operates. FDI can also be about investing in assets in a foreign country, but it is not much relevant to making a market entry unless it is a greenfield investment. It is a special type of direct foreign investment and particularly involves establishing entirely new business facilities and infrastructures from the ground up in a foreign country, which is why it is termed greenfield to convey the idea of developing on land that has not been used previously. However, greenfield investment is not relevant if the company does not require physical infrastructures, such as factories and warehouses, other than having its headquarter located in the country where it conducts business. Entering a foreign market with FDI should be considered only if other market entry methods are not possible, as it holds high risks in various aspects and requires a large sum of capital.

Except direct foreign investment, other market entry methods such as franchising, joint venture, strategic partnership, etc. are commonly considered for entering into a new market where the company has not previously operated regardless of whether it is in a foreign country or in the home country. Besides considering an appropriate market entry method, recognising the right timing of market entry also equally matters. If a company enters a market as an early entrant, it can be among the first to establish a recognised presence in the market and attempt to capture a significant market share which would later be difficult for late entrants to take away. Despite having a chance to learn from the first movers, it may however face high risks associated with considerable uncertainty about market acceptance and growth potentials. If, in contrast, the company enters late enough for a market to be mature, it will have to deal with the competition that is intense enough for it to be defeated easily unless it can successfully differentiate its products to be offered in the market.

However, late entrants can gain a chance to capitalise on the groundwork of the first movers as well as early entrants and may enter the market more effectively and efficiently with much lesser risks. At the end of the day, a path carved is the path proven.

One Indication of Lagging Behind

A business organisation should put significant effort to look ahead of the current trend and manage to have insights into possible future trends. Only then can it anticipate changes in its respective industry and adapt to them as early and easily as possible. Adapting to changes is necessary, else it will be left behind especially if the industry in which it operates is competitive and dynamic in nature. Whenever a significant change rises in the industry, the level of competition rises. Not involving in industry competition can result in threats such as loss of market share, inability to scale, risk of obsolescence, and so on. Sometimes, the organisation might be stuck in the state of equilibrium at which only little growth can be expected and no sign of dramatic growth is seen. This is referred to as strategic drift, generally indicating that it is left behind in a changing environment for being unable to keep pace after episodes of sustained achievement. One antidote to strategic drift is innovation for creating greater values. Another one is to take a precaution against getting locked in strategic drift by regularly monitoring internal forces within the organisation as well as external forces from the industry so as to give an appropriate action-oriented or goal-oriented response to them in time. Action-oriented response prioritises swift execution over extensive planning by taking practical steps towards quick results, whereas goal-oriented response prioritises strategic execution by systematically planning to achieve SMART goals (Specific, Measurable, Achievable, Relevant, and Time-bound goals). In the event of experiencing strategic drift, the organisation needs to devise and develop a strategy in line with the need to remove strategic drift and grow more. In this regard, strategy development usually happens to be a reactive process rather than a proactive one because it is intended to respond to what has happened rather than to prepare for what is likely to happen. In terms of focus, strategy development can be outside-in or inside-out. When external forces (e.g. industry disruptions, changes in economic climate, social and cultural shifts, demographic changes, competition, supply chain dynamics, technological advances, globalisation, etc.) drive a need for a strategy to be developed in response, such strategy development should be outside-in so that the organisation can be in an outward-facing position to face external challenges such as a shift in the market trends, recent customer preferences, competitor actions, emerging opportunities or threats, et cetera. Unlike this, inside-out strategy development is driven by internal forces to a need for a strategy. Internal forces include resource availability, conditions of financial health, ability to innovate, threshold of capacity, level of capability, operational performance, company growth, changes in leadership, and so on. Leveraging on internal strengths and core competencies, inside-out strategy development focuses on creating more value or enhancing the existing values not only for internal stakeholders but also for external stakeholders (especially, for customers). Strategy development is contextual by nature, but the need for staying responsive to both external and internal forces is relevant to all contexts.

Stakeholders and a Change Project

A change is inevitable. A business organisation typically faces many uncertainties, but one certainty that it undeniably has to deal with is a change. It can be led by external factors, internal factors, or a combination of both. When a change is necessary for a company within, it should be brought in systematically. In the event of approaching a change of any significance haphazardly, chaos may occur unnecessarily. If a change to be handled is significant enough, it should be undertaken as a change project such that there would be a structured effort for a difference to be made in response to driving needs for the change. A change project is meant to transition from the current state to a desired state by tackling a challenge in response or on purpose. Ideally if everybody in the organisation, particularly the stakeholders affected or concerned, accepts the change required and harmoniously works on it, a change project would be simple. In practice, a change project is typically not simple enough and is often fraught with resistance to the adoption of the change. Unless handled properly, resistance can be turned into a conflict.

Initiating a change project should start with gaining acceptance from stakeholders regardless of whether they are directly affected or indirectly concerned. In the event of signalling resistance, they should be engaged so as to reach an agreement. Motives of resistance need to be taken into account so that resistance can better be addressed. If resistance is due to lack of information or misinformation, then it can be overcome by providing accurate, complete information to the stakeholders. If resistance is owing to conflict interests, a mechanism should be established such that it encourages open dialogue and whoever perceives the change as a threat to their interests can voice their concerns so that there can be a chance to align interests and convince of the change being necessary for the organisation. If resistance is because of low tolerance for change, it can be addressed by breaking down the change into smaller, manageable steps so as to make it seem comfortable and hence lower the resistance. If resistance is based upon interpersonal conflicts, it would be difficult to handle but mediating can help have interpersonal issues sorted out a great deal. If resistance is habitual, it can be weakened by subtly giving awareness so as to remind oneself that the resistance is being driven by habitual response to the change. Basically, resistance can be effectively reduced if stakeholders feel that they are a part of change but not a driver of change.

Business leaders, particularly ones who propose a change and organise it, should conduct stakeholder analysis to understand stakeholders. Understanding each stakeholder may not be practically possible, particularly if there are too many stakeholders in an organisation. If so, understanding them in categories would help a great deal. There are three vital stakeholder categories without which a business organisation cannot survive: shareholders/investors, employees (managers and non-managers), and customers. As for shareholders and investors, they have a financial stake in the organisation and expect to receive a financial return on their investments. Managers and non-managers are both employees, each having a stake in the organisation for their livelihood. Customers are a super stakeholder category, expecting to receive a value for which they spend their money on products and/or services that the business offers. Stakeholder analysis should encompass the evaluation of the following which are helpful to understand the stakeholders as much as possible; they are their attitude, interests, needs, power, influence, and impact:

Attitude

Stakeholders' opinions matter. Their views towards the particular change brought upon by the project ought to be healthy and their stance can range from highly supporting to strongly opposing. Their attitudes can be learned through behavioural and communication indicators which include tone of voice, body language such as facial expressions and gestures, choice of words, response patterns, level of participation, consistency of actions and words spoken, micro-expressions, interaction styles (cooperative, confrontational, passive, etc.), and so on.

Interests

Depending on how well the outcomes of the change project serve the stakeholders' interests, the level of their interests in the change would vary. The better their interests would be served, the higher interest they would have in the change. It is a general rule, but an exception is that there can also be some stakeholders whose interests are high for some reason out of self-interest.

Needs

Different stakeholders have different corresponding needs to the change. As for the management, they need to ensure the alignment of the change with the organisation. Besides this, they also need resources for the change, results out of it, and other stakeholders' buy-in. As for the employees, they need to clearly understand what the change is about, why it is needed, and how it would affect their role and job security. They also need to be provided with support, transparent information, chances to voice their concern as well as to ask questions, updates about the change, and reassurance. As for suppliers and partners, they need to be informed of the change if it directly affects operational coordination, mutual benefits, or the ongoing relationships. If the change also affects consumers and customers, they need to be clearly communicated on how the change would generally affect them in terms of convenience, products, and/or services. Managing needs takes up a portion of project success and hence needs to be paid close attention.

Power

Each stakeholder has power of any degree, no matter whether it is great or a little. Powerful stakeholders such as the management typically hold higher power and hence can highly influence the change. Despite this, the collective power of non-powerful stakeholders altogether can also wield enormous power although each individual power may be limited. If the direction of the power of both groups is not the same and non-powerful stakeholders do not create the collective power, then powerful stakeholders will prevail. This is usually a default setting. However, power dynamics can also be between any stakeholders, not just between powerful stakeholders and non-powerful stakeholders.

Influence

It is generally perceived that powerful stakeholders can exert great influence on the change, where influence affects thoughts, attitudes, and even behaviours of others. In fact, influence can exist independently of power despite having a strong relation between them. Regardless of power, each stakeholder can not only influence but also be influenced. Except apex stakeholders who are not only highly tolerant to influence but also can greatly influence others, other stakeholders are subject to influence to a certain degree. Typically, managers are primary stakeholders. Although their influence may not be as strong as that of apex stakeholders, they are still good at influencing others and are also subject to influence. Stakeholders whose influence is weaker than primary stakeholders are called secondary stakeholders. They can be influenced easily and also have influence over basal stakeholders as well as neutral stakeholders who are yet undecided sometimes. Opposite to apex stakeholders, basal stakeholders are most likely to be influenced and have only a little capacity to influence others.

Impact

When stakeholders' two levels of interest (high and low) and two degrees of power (high and low) are mapped on the Mendelow Matrix, their impacts can be gauged indirectly. Mapping so gives four stakeholder groups. They are LP-LI (Low Power, Low Interest), LP-HI (Low Power, High Interest), HP-HI (High Power, High Interest), and HP-LI (High Power, Low Interest):

- LP-LI group can impact with minimal intensity, consisting of basal stakeholders and neutral stakeholders who are both okay to stay uninvolved in a state of affairs.
- LP-HI group can have low impact which can potentially intensify by forming an alliance with the other stakeholder groups, especially with HP-LI group.
- HP-LI group has moderate impact, but their impact can be as high as HP-HI group if their interest ascends for some reason.
- HP-HI group can impact with maximal intensity, consisting of apex stakeholders.

Stakeholders' interest, unless of apex stakeholders, can fluctuate between high and low, depending on circumstances and influence exerted. Interest influences the likelihood that stakeholders would exercise their respective power, and power generally influences impact. Basically the greater the power is, the greater the impact will be; the higher the level of interest is, the more likely the power is to be exercised.

Once conducted, the stakeholder analysis should be updated from time to time throughout the change project because there could be potential shifts in stakeholder influence and/or possible changes in stakeholder interests. Well understanding the stakeholders is necessary for the change project to be successful and helps increase its chance of success. In particular, the role of managers is significant enough to be a key player because they can act as a catalyst for it to proceed. They should regularly arouse the enthusiasm of secondary stakeholders, neutral stakeholders, and basal stakeholders, talking them into supporting the change and inviting more of their contributions to the change project. Their strategic influence is strong enough, but it would be stronger if they could inspire them to be more impactful. Sometimes, managers bring up a necessary change which is obvious enough to propose it to the management. Sometimes, the management brings up a change and delegates to its managers in bringing about the change. Sometimes if a change is to do with steering the course of organisation in a slightly different direction, the management itself involves and works together with the managers on the change.

Effective communication is required at all stages of the change project. Before there is communication about the change, there should be visualisation of its preferable outcomes. This would automatically guide what to communicate, how to communicate, when to communicate, whom to communicate in sequence, and with what tone of communication. Needing to be ensured that the stakeholders clearly understand about the change and the purpose, they need to be communicated as effectively as possible such that the communication is clear, consistent, targeted, compelling, persuasive, and powerful. Words used in the communication should be unambiguous enough not to be misinterpreted nor misunderstood. Communicators should also note the stakeholders' preference of how they would like to be communicated. For instance, those who are active listeners tend to understand better and quicker if they are communicated verbally; whereas, those who have a habit of giving deeper thoughts to what is being said in the moment may take a bit longer to understand promptly and tend to prefer written communication for the availability of more time to digest. Therefore, about the change project should be communicated both verbally and in writing such that the recipients understand on the same ground although the level of understanding may vary from one to another. Depending on context and amount of information to be conveyed, written communication should either be first or follow the verbal communication and vice versa. Commonly, the combination of presentation method and email communication is used to communicate about the change project. The point is to persuade into supporting the change as well as cooperating in a compelling way by delivering a simple message in the form of a story which captures attention with surprises and also evokes emotion, providing concrete examples, and using credible sources. Compelling communication itself can be persuasive enough; but if needed, appropriately using ethos (ethical appeal), pathos (emotional appeal), and logos (logical appeal) can make the persuasion stronger. Only when communication is successful can it contribute to the success chance of the change project. Successful communication is effective, compelling, and persuasive as best as possible.

It is typical that a conflict may happen during the change project. Business leaders should be proactive such that they should figure out a few practical ways ahead to manage and resolve potential conflicts concerning the change project, in case a conflict may arise or resistance turns into a conflict. In order to be capable of being proactive, they should beware of any stakeholder resistance at every stage of the change project and should try to manage it as proactively as possible so as to prevent it from getting stronger and progressing further. When conflict takes place, stakeholder engagement also becomes difficult to establish due to some disconnection in stakeholder relationships; it can also escalate unless resolved in time or left unresolved. Upon assessing the conflict and reflecting on the situation, change project leaders should throw heart and soul into having a constructive dialogue and reconnecting the relationships as quickly as possible. Negotiation and gaining mutual understanding should be the first choice regardless of whether the nature of conflict is soft or intense, involving communication effort aiming at collectively finding a solution to work on an outcome which is beneficial to the parties involved in the conflict. To initiate a process of negotiation, there should be a visualisation of outcomes intended to achieve such that the stakeholders concerned are likely to feel okay to accept them in the end. And then open the negotiation and invite the parties associated with the conflict to a formal discussion in order to find a common ground on which their interest can be established, letting them vent out how they each feel about the situation and the conflict. Upon the discussion, the negotiator then summaries what is agreed, what remains undecided, and what is disagreed. Unless mutual agreement is achieved during the discussion, another round should be scheduled to continue working on what remains unresolved. A negotiation should not be discouraged just because it was unsuccessful in the first attempt; it is common that a successful negotiation takes rounds of discussion. Following each attempt, the intended outcomes should be updated in line with the current circumstances. Commonly, soft conflict can be settled by means of negotiation. But if the negotiation does not work and the nature of the conflict becomes intense, strong intervention will be required. While strong intervention can be so effective that it can reach the resolution quickly and untangle the deadlock of the situation, it should be considered only after attempting the negotiation unsuccessfully: because it can have repercussions such as damage to relationships, perception of unfairness or bias, risk of potentially intensifying pushback, and so on. Strong intervention is necessary when the conflict persists but the change project must inevitably go on.

Not limited to a change project, stakeholders can collectively be a strong force that drives the business forward, or that bars it from moving forward, or that drags it backward. What kind of force that the stakeholders could become depends upon stakeholder relationships. As a positive, strong force collectively, healthy relationships not only bear fruit but also effectively prevent conflict and help the change project succeed forward. They play a strategic role and so they are not something that can be materialised overnight as much as a change can be spontaneous. Since development of loyal relationships within and outside matters both now and in the future, business organisations should recognise the importance of stakeholder relationships and work on them as much as possible and as early as possible.

Social and Cultural Considerations of Conducting Business

Social influences and culture can affect a business in many ways. Regardless of whether a business is conducted in a domestic or in an overseas market, it is recommended that social and cultural dimensions are considered as much as possible. In the local context of an overseas market, there should be social and cultural considerations of at least the following including but not limited to: gestures, courtesy, use of language, cross-cultural communication, and organisational culture. Not engaging in cultural appreciation may result in unhealthy public perceptions, poor relationships, operational inefficiencies, miscommunications, misunderstandings, and many other negative errors. Take the following for example:

- Bowing is an expected greeting etiquette in some countries. If, for instance, handshake greeting etiquette in such countries, it could be considered disrespectful against the local courtesy.
- In Sri Lanka, swinging head in a few side-to-side motions generally means an affirmative response. In the event of not hiring local people nor understanding this correctly, there would be communication errors in engaging with

customers.
- In Denmark, the quality of life is prioritised with an emphasis on work-life balance. In line with this, the typical full-time workweek is set at 37 hours and hence full-time staff cannot be expected to work more than 37 hours per week.
- In Spain, the afternoon break is famously long and it is common that people take a siesta in the early afternoon. Ignoring this can create a disconnection from the local culture, potentially leading to a tension between foreign employers and their local employees.

Alongside cultural appreciation, organisational culture should also be in line with the local workplace culture of the territory in which a business operates. Being a set of values and behaviours that creates a vibe of its working environment, organisational culture guides the actions of all members belonging to the organisation. Regarding this, Charles Handy – a pre-eminent management thinker – suggested the four types of culture. They are power culture, task culture, person culture, and role culture:

> Power culture

Power culture is hierarchical. In this culture, only very few individuals at the top levels of the organisation hold power and inferior employees have to follow strict rules. This means that power in such organisations is unequally distributed due to centralised power and hierarchical control. In the event of adopting power culture, leadership can be strong but very authoritative.

Task culture

Task culture emphasises on equal contribution to getting work done. In this culture, success is measured by the completion of tasks. This means that the focus is on the execution of tasks. In the event of adopting task culture, everybody has to be task-oriented. Task culture may rather be preferred in teams, start-ups, and small organisations than in big organisations despite the fact that it can be integrated into another organisational culture and coexists.

Role culture

With a lesser degree, role culture can be said to be an integrated version of both power culture and task culture. In this culture, everybody is expected to play a role in a distinct boundary within which they are highly expected not only to perform and execute tasks as defined by the role but also to be accountable and responsible for their actions associated with their respective role. Power culture may persist but is not dominant.

Person culture

Person culture emphasises on individuals and their development. Business organisations that adopt person culture are people-oriented, thus in this culture people are greatly valued to the extent that they care about their people's self-progression in parallel to the organisational progress at the expense of some collective values. Business may suffer, and hence rarely do business organisations adopt person culture unless they have a specific mission, for example, for the development of society, communities, etc.

In the aspect of communication, how people with different cultural backgrounds communicate should be taken into account. Regarding cross-cultural communication, Edward T. Hall – an influential anthropologist and cross-cultural researcher – introduced the two communication cultures. They are high-context culture and low-context culture:

- High-context communication culture implies indirect, implicit communication and heavily relies not only on context but also on unspoken information substantially conveyed. It is polychronic and relationship-oriented. Verbal communication is preferred to written communication. The response of communication is frequently based on intuition and feelings. Take Mexico's communication culture for example.
- Low-context communication culture implies direct, explicit communication and heavily relies on words. It is monochronic and typically expects commitment to words. Written communication is preferred to verbal communication. The response of communication is based on facts and evidence. Following rules and standards is highly expected. Take Germany's communication culture for example.

The culture of a country is also influential to the extent that it can overwhelm or dictate organisational cultures and communication cultures. Geert Hofstede's six cultural dimensions can be used for the considerations of national culture, namely power distance, indulgence versus restraint, uncertainty avoidance, individualism versus collectivism, long-term versus short-term orientation, and masculinity versus femininity:

Power distance

Power distance is the degree to which the society can accept the unequal distribution of power. Power distance can be low, high, or in between. High power distance means high acceptance of power inequality in the society and low power distance means the reverse. Thus, power culture is compatible with high power distance society.

Indulgence versus restraint

Indulgence society emphasises on pursuing happiness and leading life to gratification, whereas restrained culture emphasises work over gratification. Thus, task culture is more congruent with restrained culture than indulgence society.

Uncertainty avoidance

Uncertainty avoidance is to do with the degree of tendency towards uncertainty and the extent to which society feels uncomfortable about uncertainty. High uncertainty avoidance indicates that society highly expects certainty, whereas low uncertainty avoidance indicates that society can tolerate uncertainty. Ideally, UAI = 0 means that society is perfectly happy to tolerate uncertainty. Society with a strong tendency towards high uncertainty avoidance would prefer role culture because it is perceived to have clarity, stability, prolonged efficiency, and predictability, etc. which all feature a sense of certainty.

Individualism versus collectivism

Individualistic society places greater emphasis on the sense of self and hence ties between one another in the society are weak enough to care about others, whereas collectivist society prefers the sense of community and ties between the members of society are strong enough to care and help others. Thus, person culture is oriented towards individualistic society and task culture is relevant to collectivist society.

Long-term versus short-term orientation

Society with long-term orientation has tolerance for delay in gratification, appreciating sustained effort, perseverance, thriftiness, and patience. Conversely, society with short-term orientation puts an emphasis on the link between the past and the present, prioritising quick results and immediate gratification. Neither long-term orientation nor short-term orientation in society does not much affect the organisational culture of business organisations not only because they may have to be either long-term oriented or short-term oriented depending on the nature of business but also because they may have to switch their orientation under circumstances.

Masculinity versus femininity

Masculine society values open behaviours, clarity, assertiveness, and effectiveness, thus low-context communication aligns with masculine society. In contrast, feminine society values empathy, harmony, diplomacy, and collaboration. Thus, high-context communication is in sync with feminine society.

Whatever culture a business organisation may choose to internally nurture, it is important that the choice is consistent with both national and local values of the market in which it operates. Conducting business internationally or globally, it is likely that there would be social and cultural barriers. Nevertheless, they can be overcome by means of social and cultural considerations. Regarding this, take Kentucky Fried Chicken (KFC) for example. KFC is a long-lasting brand and has massive experience of entering into international markets. Every time it enters an international market, it adapts to the local culture and satisfies local customers as much as possible by making efforts of throwing heart and soul into serving local preference such as offering local cuisine and local taste. Take KFC in Shanghai for instance: KFC Shanghai branches offer porridge on the breakfast menu and Peking duck burgers on the lunch menu. This is referred to as a glocal strategy [a combination of 'global' and 'local']. By adopting the glocal strategy, KFC earns acceptance from local people, which helps weaken social and cultural barriers to a certain extent. Thus, integrating social and cultural considerations into business conduct should be considered necessary as it can help lead to harmonious, sustainable outcomes.

Preliminary Initiation of Developing a Sustainability Strategy

Sustainability strategy refers to a plan that is intended to achieve meeting the needs of people and financial goals of business organisations by taking account of any impact on the environment, integrating the balance of not only profitability but also environmental and social considerations into the operations and decision-making of a business organisation. In a nutshell, there have to be the three pillars which support a sustainability strategy: social needs, profit, and the environment. At the end of the day, a sustainability strategy should be for attaining sustainable development. In 1987, the United Nations Brundtland Commission defined sustainable development as one "that meets the needs of the present without compromising the ability of future generations to meet their own needs". This definition can be used as the benchmark against which the outcomes of a sustainability strategy can be measured. Unless its outcomes satisfy the definition, it can be said that the strategy does not fully orient towards strategy development and may need to be reconsidered.

Developing a sustainability strategy should be regarded as a holistic process but not an isolated one. In other words, sustainability should not be treated as a separate or secondary initiative to avoid fragmented efforts and should be given coordinated efforts. Regarding this, considering whether or not integrating sustainability into a business organisation's long-term strategies and core business functions could be challenging. Being a substantial decision to make, it would need many rounds of in-depth discussion and might take time to reach the conclusion. If there has already been widespread acceptance of sustainability within the organisation, it would help a great deal in reaching the agreement.

To develop a sustainability strategy, business leaders should start with identifying and justifying reasons to formulate sustainability as well as striking a balance between its organisational benefits and risks of not engaging in sustainability. This is often referred to as a business case for sustainability. Upon creating the case, it should be communicated with the stakeholders effectively because their acceptance matters in order for a sustainability strategy to be successful. Regarding sustainability efforts, business leaders should consider the following including but not limited to: increasing sales in line with CSR, making products more environmental-friendly, reducing carbon footprint, raising public awareness about environmental issues, enhancing the brand image with sustainability activities, integrating operational efficiency with sustainability, and helping improve the life quality of the employees. For the sake of consistency, sustainability needs to be embedded in all functions of the business.

Identifying impact areas for which sustainability goals are to be defined, business leaders need to work on defining sustainability goals and make sure such goals reflect the vision and mission statements of the business organisation. One way to identify such impact areas is by mapping business activities undertaken along its value chain in which a value is added at each stage. Once mapped, sustainability goals can be defined in order of significance of the impact areas identified. If, for instance, high-energy consumption is identified as one impact area, then a sustainability goal can be defined as one that is to reduce the energy consumption by 5% next year by adopting energy-efficient practices. It is important that such sustainability goals defined are effective such that they would, as intended, lessen and weaken sustainability stains in the value chain if they are achieved. To be meaningful, sustainability goals should be SMART, i.e. Specific, Measurable, Achievable, Realistic, and Time-bound. When they are achieved, their outcomes should be checked against what the sustainability strategy intends, e.g. satisfying the sustainable development definition of the United Nations Brundtland Commission, satisfying the triangle of the environment, the needs of people, and business profit is satisfied, etc. In essence, a sustainability strategy should be bold, transformative, and enduring.

Corporate Social Responsibility Models

Corporate Social Responsibility (CSR) is an ethos by which businesses take account of their impact on the society and the environment with the aim to attain sustainability and long-term success. Business organisations practising CSR not only transcend the traditional aim of maximising profits but also contribute positively to societal and environmental goals, understanding that CSR activities can enhance their brand reputations which foster customer loyalty as well as the trust of their stakeholders. Some business organisations may have their policies in place for CSR and formulate their own model, in which way various core principles can be applied for best effect. Or, CSR models can be adopted in order to structure and implement CSR efforts, providing guidelines on how businesses can address social and environmental responsibilities in a sustainable way. Many CSR models are available for use; but by analysing their core principles, one that is a best fit for the organisational ethos should be appropriately selected. Common models of corporate social responsibility are Archie Carroll's pyramid model, and economic model, philanthropic model. In general, CSR models encourage business organisations to be far-sighted to a greater extent that they should also take account of whoever is affected by their business activities in managing their business affairs for the sake of serving the shareholders.

Archie Carroll's pyramid model approaches CSR in the four interconnected aspects in terms of responsibilities: economic, legal, ethical, and philanthropic. Its core principle is based on society's expectations of businesses. At the base of the pyramid, society primarily expects businesses to remain running and profitable for economic growth and sustainability at local, regional, or national level. In other words, society chiefly expects businesses to take economic responsibility. On top of economic responsibility, society requires businesses to comply with legal regulations. Climbing up the pyramid, society expects businesses to be ethically responsible such that they are fair and do what is right. Nevertheless, whether or not being ethical is not an obligation for businesses but an option. Therefore, businesses can only be influenced to feel compelled to take ethical responsibilities as much as possible. At the apex of the pyramid is philanthropy. Society highly appreciates businesses for any activity that improves the quality of society and the welfare of its people in the form of giving back to communities that they serve and probably beyond, but nevertheless philanthropy is only voluntary and ought not to be expected that there always will be.

Economic model of CSR states that a business fulfils social responsibility as long as it fulfils the economic function(s) that they choose to serve, recognising that such economic duty of a business is its fundamentally sole duty. This model holds the concept of economy and follows economic theory as its core principles, being compatible with the nature of business organisations. This encourages businesses to pursue the focal goal of maximising profit and increasing shareholder value within the legal frameworks by adhering to regulations and ethical norms. Milton Friedman, a renowned economist and Sveriges Riksbank Prize winner, also argued for this concept and pointed out that using company funds for charity disturbs profit maximisation despite adding shareholder value. This model perceives that social activities are not in line with economic theory and thus businesses are not supposed nor responsible for supporting charity causes, discouraging businesses supporting activism of any sort.

Philanthropic model of CSR can be said to be an integrated version of CSR economic model in a way that exhibits altruistic behaviours and encourages businesses to engage in philanthropic projects, in addition to their economic business activities. The core principle of this model is based on altruistic motives. In order for businesses to be philanthropic, they first have to be capable. To be capable in a philanthropic way, they need to be rich in time, effort, or money. If, for instance, they have time and effort only but not much profit, they ought to consider volunteerism or in-kind contributions; if they are highly profitable, they should consider charitable contributions. If they have time, effort, and money, they may drive a societal cause for greater good. Therefore, the more capable a business organisation is, the greater they can be philanthropic. Above all, it takes altruism to be philanthropic.

In order to ensure that CSR efforts are effective, they should be benchmarked against Triple Bottom Line (TBL) sustainability which, in other words, is the bottom line of sustainability that business organisations ought to achieve in the three dimensions (social, environmental, and economic) at least. TBL sustainability can be approached with CSR policy. To develop one, the following steps may be taken: 1) Conducting CSR assessment, 2)

Developing CSR strategy, 3) Implementing CSR commitments, as defined in the strategy, to TBL sustainability, 4) CSR reporting on TBL sustainability, and 5) Monitoring and evaluating for improvement. Now let us take Patagonia for example regarding its CSR commitments to TBL sustainability. It is a renowned American outdoor clothing and gear company. Established in 1973, Patagonia has been on the way to TBL sustainability as early as possible and has implemented its CSR commitments along the way. Some of them can be given as examples below:

- Patagonia launched the campaign "The responsible economy" regarding the sparing use of natural resources before their disposal.
- Regarding support actions on pressing environmental issues, Patagonia has created the network named Patagonia Action Work with the purpose to connect environmental groups and has also taken part for nearly forty years in supporting grassroots groups for problem-solving regarding the environmental crisis.
- Regarding the commitment to the use of environmental-friendly materials in making its products, Patagonia is also environmentally responsible in a way that it uses not only environmental-friendly materials but also recycled materials to reduce additional textile waste.
- Regarding the commitment to durability of its products made, Patagonia makes their products durable as long as possible, perceiving that it is their way of taking corporate social responsibility as well as making efforts not only to prevent their products from quickly going out of use due to wear and tear but also to consume less energy and less water for unnecessary production of socially irresponsible

demands.
- Patagonia launched the online store named Worn Wear to repair, trade in, and buy used Patagonia clothing and gear so that its products sold can have their lifespan prolonged without being discarded prematurely.
- Having pledged 1% of sales, since 1985, to the reservation and restoration of the natural environment, Patagonia has awarded over US$140 million in cash and in-kind donations to grassroots environmental groups.
- Patagonia has worked on living wages, incorporating its living wage standard in its code of conduct and urging its partner factories to improve wages.
- Due to the environmentally harmful nature of growing cotton conventionally, Patagonia declined the use of conventional cotton and switched to organic practices.

Patagonia's engagement in CSR is rather out of a sense of responsibility and altruistic motives than due to legal requirements. Because of its CSR commitments, consumers can feel comfortable purchasing its products without a sense of guilt about harming the environment as they can trust and recognise it as an ethical business. Patagonia has existed in business for nearly five decades during which it has shown the care for the impacts on people and the environment as much as it focuses on making profit. Being an action-oriented organisation, its devoted actions to CSR speak for themselves in the present days. Demonstrated records of evidence in meeting the triple bottom line of sustainability, its CSR efforts can be regarded as effective.

Common Business Ethical Theories: A Snapshot Overview

Business ethics are moral principles by which businesses and individuals are expected to engage in business activities. They guide the conduct of businesspeople and business organisations such that their actions are fair, responsible, and ethical (i.e. morally correct, or morally acceptable). Business ethics frameworks can be used in making ethical business decisions to ensure that business practices are aligned with moral values, social expectation, and legal standards. Not only do they provide guidelines and principles to help navigate ethical issues, but they also offer structured methods of evaluating several aspects related to ethical behaviours and decision-making. Many business ethics frameworks are available for consultation. Among them, deontological framework and teleological framework are common.

Deontological ethics is governed by non-consequentialist theories with a special emphasis on the inherent morality of actions rather than on their consequences. Given that actions are evaluated and judged right based on the underlying moral principles and/or rights of ethics, deontological ethics suggest that actions should be taken out of duty to act and be disassociated from the consideration of outcomes or consequences. On the other hand, teleological ethics is governed by consequentialist theories with a focus on the consequences of actions. Such theories suggest that an action is considered good if its corresponding outcome(s) is desirable and an action is deemed poor otherwise. Associated with outcomes, utilitarianism being a consequentialist theory states that an action is considered morally right if it causes the greatest amount of happiness for as many people as possible who are affected by it.

Take Patagonia for example regarding the use of business ethics. Established in 1973, Patagonia Inc. is a renowned American outdoor clothing and gear company. It has been known for its high-quality products, environmental activism, and sustainable business practices. Take its self-imposed Earth tax – 1% for the Planet – for example. This indicates its urge to protect the environment in a certain way guided by pre-existing principles. Its intention of 1% for the planet is no other than to protect the environment regardless of the outcomes of its action. Moreover, Patagonia has been consistent in taking some environmental responsibilities and organising environmental activism. It launched the campaign "The responsible economy" which called on consumers and businesses to consider, directly or indirectly, using natural resources sparingly before disposing. In addition to the care about the environment, Patagonia also engages in due diligence activities regarding ethical labour practices and implements workplace compliance benchmarks for their suppliers in place. These instances show Patagonia's respect for human dignity and human rights. Satisfying many underlying moral principles as well as rights of ethics, Patagonia's actions can be deemed ethical in accordance with deontological ethics.

Despite this, Patagonia does not entirely neglect the outcomes of its actions but also gives some consideration to them in a form of motivation. In terms of utilitarianism, a so-called utility has to be assigned to something and the utility assigned is supposed to cause a greatest amount of happiness. As for Patagonia, it assigns one utility to what they do, so to speak, i.e. the production of high-quality clothing and gear. Being a continual series of day-to-day actions but not a single action, it is indeed a high-commitment utility. This utility has proved that it causes a greatest amount of happiness for whoever uses its products and continues to be this way. This implies that Patagonia's day-to-day actions can be considered morally right in accordance with utilitarianism and hence generally satisfy teleological ethics.

In business industries, nearly all business organisations practise egoism and they commonly make decision(s) to serve their business interests rather than the interests of others. Being a business organisation, Patagonia might happen to practise egoism if its decision makers support action(s) taken in line with their collective decision-making in favour of its business interests. This is just the nature of a business organisation. However if business organisations care enough to be considerate towards the interests of others, enlightened egoism may be considered in taking account of non-self-interests as part of their self-interests. Enlightened egoism recognises that helping others helps serve self-interests: helping others and considering their needs benefit serving self-interests to a certain extent. Enlightened egotism is more possible than avoiding egotism.

Subtle Influences on Making Ethical Business Decisions

Ethical organisational culture refers to a set of values, beliefs, and behaviours that not only creates a vibe of its working environment but also guides the actions of its members. It should overwhelm all functions in a business organisation so as to be holistically integrated into its decision-making as well as to maintain the collective focus across all departments on meeting the triple bottom line. Besides being subjected to influences within, the local culture and/or the national culture at large can also externally influence an ethical organisational culture which in turn partially influences making ethical decisions. Sometimes, business decision-making is highly associated with ethical dilemmas to which business organisations are prone by nature. Suppose that a clothing company uses perfluorocarbons (PFCs) in producing water-repellent clothing to protect users against getting frostbite due to soaking water in the garment in extreme cold weather. Since PFCs are harmful to the environment, the company is reluctant to continue using PFCs in its production. Regarding this, the company faces a dilemma whether to terminate or continue the use of PFCs. If, for instance, its organisational culture is generally overwhelmed under the influence of the local or national culture with high Uncertainty Avoidance Index (UAI) which therefore highly expects certainty, it is not likely that the use of PFCs would be discontinued; one probable basis is that what has consistently been working over a prolonged period of time is regarded as almost certainty and disrupting it would invite unwanted uncertainty which is least preferred within such an organisational culture. At the end of the day, it is organisational culture that fosters favourable conditions for ethical leadership to thrive on by which ethical influence can best be exerted on decision-making and the ethical quality of decisions to be made can be ensured. In this way, a success chance of making ethical business decisions mediated by ethical leadership can be maximised. There are two modes of ethical leadership which approach ethical business decision-making. They are ethical cultural change and ethical cultural learning. If the company adopts ethical cultural change, the role of its leaders is to personify and embody the values and standards of the organisation in a way that inspires and motivates the employees to follow their lead. However, the effectiveness of this mode firmly ties to the leaders' morality: moral leaders are highly likely to make ethical decisions and vice versa. Whereas if the company adopts ethical cultural learning, its leaders play a significant role in guiding and enabling the employees to make ethical decisions in addition to promoting ethical behaviours within the organisation. However, this model relies on the trust that a majority of the employees could make right decisions, potentially posing risks of making decisions that happen to be unethical. Not only ethical cultural change but also ethical cultural learning takes time to be nurtured. Relevant to both modes of ethical leadership, ethical leaders need to connect the company's values to the support of its stakeholders as well as to societal legitimacy (i.e. widespread acceptance for an organisation within the society at large). This commonly implies that ethical leaders should demonstrate how the goods and/or services that the company offers make positive and non-negative contributions not only to its stakeholders but also to the broader communities it serves, thereby enhancing overall reputation and trustworthiness for the company.

www.ingramcontent.com/pod-product-compliance
Lightning Source LLC
Chambersburg PA
CBHW030459220526
45464CB00006B/2583